OUR AMAZING WORLD
DINOSAURS

Kay de Silva

Aurora

Contents

A Tarbosaurus prowling along the water's edge.

DINOSAURS

Dinosaurs roamed the earth for a period of 180 million years. This was during the *Mesozoic Era*, which was known as the *Age of Reptiles*. The dinosaur was one of many *pre-historic* animals that lived at the time. The word dinosaur means *scary lizard*.

FOSSILS

Dinosaurs were around long before people. So, how do we know what dinosaurs looked like and how they lived? *Fossils* give us clues. Fossils are the preserved remains of plants and animals and their activities.

There are two types of fossils. The first is *body fossils*, which are the preserved remains of a plant or animal. The second is *trace fossils*, which are the remains of the activities of animals. These include footprints, track marks, fossilized egg shells and nests.

Paleontologists study fossils to learn about the pre-historic world. This study is known as *paleontology*. Then, like detectives, paleontologists use all the clues they have to recreate what dinosaurs looked like and understand how they behaved millions of years ago.

An effigy of a Tyrannosaurus skeleton embedded in a mountain side.

ANATOMY

The dinosaur was neither a reptile nor a bird. It was, however, closely related to both. It is said that dinosaurs evolved from *cold-blooded* reptiles to being *warm blooded animals*, like the birds of today.

Dinosaurs also had a unique hip structure that allowed them to walk upright. The first dinosaurs walked on two legs (bi-pedal). Later some dinosaurs began to walk on all fours (quadrupedal). Even then, generally their front legs remained shorter than their back legs.

There are many types of dinosaurs, but the two main types are the *Sauropod* and the *Theropod*. Sauropods had four legs and Theropods had two.

A ferocious Tyrannosaurus roaring in a jungle.

HABITAT

All dinosaurs did not live at the same time, nor did they live in the same place. During different periods dinosaurs lived in different parts and habitats around the world. Dinosaurs lived during three main periods in the Mesozoic era: *Triassic*, *Jurassic* and *Cretaceous*.

The Triassic period was the first period which was 250 to 200 million years ago. At the time it is believed that the world was joined together as a single *super-continent* called *Pangaea*. This continent was so huge that the inland areas were far away from the ocean. This created vast deserts in the middle of the continent. During this period dinosaurs lived near *riversides* and *scrublands*.

200 to 145 million years ago, during the Jurassic period, Pangaea began to break up. This was believed to have been caused by volcanic eruptions. Shallow seas emerged and spread across former deserts. This resulted in damper climates and more *vegetation* being created. During this time dinosaurs' primary habitats were forests.

During the Cretaceous period, 145 to 65 million years ago, the continents had broken apart further. They began to look like the continents of today. The different land areas created different climates. Groups of dinosaurs that looked different to each other emerged across different continents. At this time dinosaurs lived in swamplands, mixed forests, mountains and desert plains.

A mother Brachiosaurus guiding her young to an island habitat.

SENSES

Understanding how a dinosaur's senses worked is difficult. This is because the parts that make up its brain has not fossilized well.

It is said that the *Hadrosaurus* (had-ro-SAWR-us) or the *duckbilled dinosaur* made lots of sounds and had a good sense of hearing. To make a noise it used a flap of skin over its broad beak, just like the throat-pouch of a bullfrog does.

The *Parasaurolophus* (PARR-uh-SAWR-uh-LOH-fus) had a crest which was made up of tubes connected to its nostrils. Blowing air through these tubes would have made a noise, which would have sounded much like a trombone.

The *Troodon* (TRUE-oh-don) was a turkey-sized carnivore with binocular vision. It had eyes that pointed forward and a brain as large as an emu's. This gave it the brain power to see three-dimensional images that it received using its binocular vision.

Sauropods such as the *Triceratops* (try-SER-uh-tops) had eyes on the side of its head. This gave it a wide field of vision, which allowed it to quickly scan the landscape for danger and defend itself in time.

Notice the Albertaceratop's wide-set eyes.

MOVEMENT

Dinosaurs usually walked on their toes (digitigrade). Digitigrade animals of today include cats, dogs and chickens. A pad on the back of these animals feet act as shock absorbers. Humans, bears and crocodiles on the other hand walk flat-footed (plantigrade).

Depending on their anatomy some dinosaurs moved on all fours and others on two legs. A third type ran on two legs and grazed on fours. Some were swift while others were slow. A few bird-like dinosaurs may have used their feathered arms to speed up their running and possibly glide from trees to the ground.

Paleontologists used footprints to understand the movements of dinosaurs. Using these prints they were able to tell the structure of the animal's foot, the number of toes the dinosaur had, whether there were pads on its feet and if it was plantigrade or not.

They were also able to tell how many legs the dinosaur had. Using the distance between prints and the length of its legs they were able to work out how fast the animal moved.

A dinosaur footprint preserved in a river-bed.

FEEDING

Sauropods were *herbivores* (plant eaters). They were usually slow moving. They had four columnar legs and a long neck for grazing. They had long tails to counter-balance their long neck. These creatures had tiny heads and small brains.

Plant eaters had blunt teeth which were useful in stripping vegetation (leaves and twigs). Some animals had flat teeth to grind plant fibers. Many dinosaurs had cheek pouches to store food. They also had to eat a lot to get their fill.

The Theropod was a fast moving *carnivore* (flesh eater). Its head was large and neck muscular. It had two long and strong legs that gave it the ability to run and catch prey. It had short arms with deadly claws to grasp and tear apart its prey.

It also had big sharp teeth and scissor like jaws, which it used to chew and swallow its victims. It was a great hunter because of its keen eyesight and sharp sense of smell. Its big brain helped it to plan its hunt.

The carnivorous Yangchuanosaurus chasing the 'terror bird' Phorusrhacos.

A 100 million year old dinosaur egg exhibited at the University of Zurich.

EGGS

Dinosaurs, like the reptiles and birds of today hatched from eggs. These eggs came in many shapes and sizes. Some eggs were 30 centimeters (1 foot) long. They may have weighed up to 15 pounds (7 kilograms). The smallest eggs found were about 2.5 centimeters (1 inch) across. Bigger eggs did not always mean bigger dinosaurs. Some very large dinosaurs had very small eggs.

Dinosaurs are said to have laid their eggs in *clutches* (groups) of a few or a few dozen. Some dinosaurs cared for their eggs; others hid them away from *predators*. There were also those who simply laid their eggs and walked away.

Allosaurus at sunset.

ALLOSAURUS

Allosaurus (al-uh-SAWR-us) means *strange lizard*. It is known as such because its backbone was different to other dinosaurs.

The average length of the Allosaurus was 8.5 meters (28 feet) and it weighed about 2.5 tons (2,300 kilograms). It was a Theropod. It would eat other dinosaurs and *carcasses*. With its razor sharp teeth and hooked claws it was a killing machine. It would grab its victims with its fore-arms and wound it with its terrible claws. It would then tear off chunks of its prey's flesh with its teeth.

At the time it lived these dinosaurs were known as *apex-predators*. As such, they were on top of the food chain. This means that they had no predators of their own.

The Allosaurus belonged to the Jurassic period. Fossils of this dinosaur have been found in North America, Tanzania, Portugal and Australia.

BRACHIOSAURUS

The *Brachiosaurus* (brack-ee-oh-SAWR-us) is the largest and heaviest land animal to ever have roamed the earth. Brachiosaurus means *arm reptile*. It was given this name because of its front legs, which are longer than its back legs.

This dinosaur was around 26 meters (85 feet) long and weighed 40 tons (36,300 kilograms). It could reach up to a height of 9 meters (30 feet). This is as tall as two double-decker buses stacked on top of each other.

The Brachiosaurus was a *Sauropod*. Like a giraffe it fed on leaves of trees high above the ground. So it is known as a *high feeder*. It had spoon-shaped teeth that were useful for its leafy diet. It is said that it needed to eat about 440 to 880 pounds (200 to 400 kilograms) of food every day.

The Brachiosaurus lived in the Jurassic period. The fossils of these dinosaurs have been found in Colorado, other parts of North America, Africa, Europe, Portugal and Tanzania.

A Brachiosaurus strolling on to shore.

DEINONYCHUS

Deinonychus (DIE-no-ni-kus) means *terrible claw*. This refers to this dinosaur's large sickle-shaped claw found on the second toe of each hind foot. This dinosaur has *retractable* claws. This means that like a cat it could pull its claws into a sheath when not in use. In this way it protected its valuable *weapon* from being dragged along the ground, catching or becoming blunt.

The Deinonychus was a Theropod. It was a relatively small dinosaur that grew to be about 1 meter (3 feet) tall, 3.5 meters (11 feet) in length and weighed about 170 pounds (75 kilograms).

This dinosaur was the size of a small car, but is known as the *world's deadliest dinosaur*. It attacked its prey in multiple ways. The Deinonychus had a strong tail which it used to help it balance on one foot and fight with its claws. It used its muscular legs to jump straight on to its victims and used its claws like knives to stab its prey. It also used its 60 dagger-like teeth with the bite-force of an alligator.

With the ability to move like a flightless bird this dinosaur is thought to be a close ancestor of today's birds. It would gang up with other Deinonychus dinosaurs to bring down carnivores much larger than itself including the fierce *Tyrannosaurus*.

The Deinonychus lived during the Cretaceous Period. Its fossil remains have been found in Oklahoma, Montana, Wyoming and Maryland.

A deadly Deinonychus searching for prey.

A pair of Diplodocus wading through shallow water to reach vegetation.

DIPLODOCUS

The *Diplodocus* (dih-PLAH-duh-kuss) is the longest known dinosaur. Its name means double *beamed lizard*. It gets its name from its very powerful back legs.

It was about 27 meters (88 feet) long. It weighed about 12 tons (11,000 kilograms), which is as much as a large truck. Its neck could reach over 6 meters (20 feet). As a Sauropod, its body was balanced by its long and heavy tail. Its tail was about 14 meters (46 feet) in length and had 80 *vertebrae*. This animal had the longest tail of any animal that has walked the earth.

This tail was also used as a weapon against its attackers. It was previously thought that its tail dragged along as it walked. However, no drag marks were found alongside its fossilized prints.

These dinosaurs are believed to have traveled in herds. They belonged to the Jurassic period. Their remains have been found in Colorado, Wyoming and other parts of North America.

An Elasmosaurus' long neck puts a giraffe's neck to shame.

ELASMOSAURUS

The *Elasmosaurus* (eh-laz-muh-SAWR-us) was a sea creature. It was a reptile and not a dinosaur. It could easily be spotted because of its long neck. Its neck was 7 meters (23 feet) long, which is 4 times longer than a giraffe's neck.

This reptile measured around 14 meters (46 feet) in length and weighed over 2 tons (1,800 kilograms). It was too heavy to stand. If it could, however, it would have been about 9 meters (30 feet) tall. It had a small head, sharp teeth and strong jaws.

It swam slowly in the open ocean and breathed air. It used its 4 paddle-like flippers much like the sea-turtle of today. It ate fish, molluscs, squid and other small sea creatures. The Elasmosaurus swallowed small stones to help digest its food.

This reptile lived in the Cretaceous period. Its fossils have been found in Wyoming and other parts of North America.

A Kentrosaurus walking wearily along a dry riverbed in search of food.

KENTROSAURUS

The *Kentrosaurus* (KEN-tro-SAWR-us) was a Sauropod. It was a cousin of the Stegosaurus. Like the Stegosaurus it had bony plates along its back and tail. The plates on the Kentrosaurus gradually became narrower as it reached its tail until they resembled spikes.

Kentrosaurus means *spiked lizard*. Its spikes could grow up to 0.6 meters (2 feet) long. It also had a spike on each hip. These spikes protected it from other dinosaurs such as the Allosaurus. A swish of its spiked tail was a deadly weapon against its enemies.

A Kentrosaurus grew to be about 5 meters (16 feet) in length and weighed around 2 tons (18,000 kilograms). Belonging to the late Jurassic period, its remains have been found in North America and some parts of Africa.

A Peteinosaurus taking to the skies.

PETEINOSAURUS

The *Peteinosaurus* (PET-in-uh-SAWR-us) was one of the first flying reptiles that was closely related to the dinosaur. It was also one of the first *vertebrates* (creatures with a backbone) that could fly rather than glide. This gave the creature its name, which means *winged lizard.*

The Peteinosaurus was a mere 4 ounces (100 grams), which is the weight of an onion. It had a wingspan of two feet. Its 20 centimeter (8 inch) long tail had a rudder at the end. Its wings were made up of skin stretched between a long finger in its hand and its foot. It had sharp, cone-like teeth. It is believed to have eaten insects that it found in flight.

The creature belonged to the Late Triassic period. Its fossils have been found in Western Europe.

A Plateosaurus migrating across a dry European landscape.

PLATEOSAURUS

Plateosaurus (PLAT-ee-uh-SAWR-us) means *broad lizard*. Its name was probably given to it because of its size. This dinosaur was about 27.5 feet (8 meters long) and weighed about 1,500 pounds (700 kilograms).

It had a long neck, tail and snout. It had five clawed fingers on its feet and a large thumb claw. It probably used these for walking and grasping. Its front legs were shorter than its back legs. It probably stood up on its back legs to reach high vegetation. It was one of the first long-necked herbivores.

The Plateosaurus may have lived in herds. Seasonally they would migrate across Europe, which was *arid* (extremely dry) and much like a desert at the time. These dinosaurs lived during the Triassic period.

A Pteranodon gliding across a vast ocean

PTERANODON

The *Pteranodon* (tuh-RAN-uh-don) was a massive flying reptile that lived during the same period as dinosaurs. From tip to tip their wings were about 10 meters (32 feet) long. This made it as large as a hang-glider.

This creature was about 2 meters (6 feet) long and weighed about 35 pounds (16 kilograms). It had a beak, no teeth, a short tail and a crest on its head. The crest was possibly used to counter-balance the weight of its huge beak.

Pteranodon wings were covered by a tough *membrane* (thin and flexible skin). This leathery membrane stretched between its body, the top of its legs and a long fourth finger. This formed the structure of its wings. Claws protruded from its other fingers.

It ate fish, squid and other small oceanic animals which suggests that it was a coastal animal. The Pteranodon lived in the Cretaceous period and was widely found in North America.

A Stegosaurus in a Jurassic landscape.

STEGOSAURUS

Stegosaurus (steg-uh-SAWR-us) means *roofed lizard*. It was given this name because of the large bony plates on its back which looked like roof tiles. It is believed that these plates were useful to defend it against predators. It is also thought to act as a way to control the animal's temperature.

The Stegosaurus was heavily built and strong. It was around 9 meters (30 feet) in length, 4 meters (13 feet) in height and weighed up to 2 tons (18,000 kilograms). It had a powerful tail with two *horizontal* spikes at the end of its tail. Although it had a strong body its brain was just around the size of a dog's.

This Sauropod did not have front teeth. It had a beak instead. On either side of its jaws it had tiny, weak teeth. So it enjoyed soft vegetation.

The Stegosaurus lived in the Jurassic Period. Its fossils have been found in North America and Europe.

A Tylosaurus preparing to dine.

TYLOSAURUS

Tylosaurus (tie-luh-SAWR-us) means *knob lizard*. It was given the name because of its blunt and powerful head, which it used to ram its prey. The animal was not a dinosaur, but lived around the same time. It was one of the deadliest hunters of the ancient seas.

It grew to over 14 meters (45 feet), making it one of the largest marine reptiles. It made a meal of any smaller creature that crossed its path. This included shark and other fish, seabirds and Plesiosaurus. It used its snout to locate prey. Its jaws were lined with pointed cone-shaped teeth. It gulped its prey whole. Once inside its deadly jaws, two extra rows of teeth on the roof of its mouth made escape impossible.

The Tylosaurus lived during the Cretaceous period and had few natural predators. Its fossilized remains were found widely in the shallow seas of Central America.

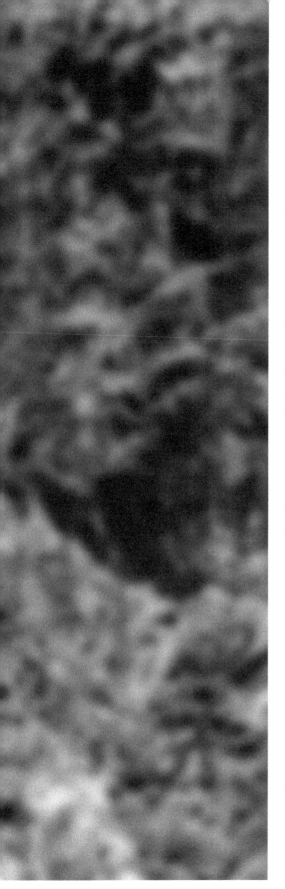

TYRANNOSAURUS

The Tyrannosaurus (tie-ran-uh-SAWR-us) or the Tyrannosaurus Rex (T-Rex) is possibly the best known dinosaur in the world. Its name means *tyrant* or *cruel lizard*. Rex means *king*. The name is well suited to this dinosaur that could eat up to 500 pounds (230 kilograms) of flesh in a single bite.

The T-Rex was one of the largest meat-eating dinosaurs. It measured 13 meters (42 feet) in length. It was about 5 meters (18 feet) tall and weighed about 7 tons (6,500 kilograms). Although it was a huge creature it moved quickly with the help of its massive thighs and long powerful tail.

This dinosaur lived during the Cretaceous period, in the forested river valleys of North America.

A Tyrannosaurus' conical teeth are used to grip and pierce its prey.

Avian dinosaurs attempting to escape the devastation.

DINOSAUR DOOMSDAY

No one really knows what caused the *extinction* of dinosaurs. So paleontologists have *theories* to explain how it happened.

Some believe it was caused by a single incident such as an asteroid that crashed on to earth during the Cretaceous period. Others believe that a massive volcano which erupted at the time caused the extinction.

There was also the theory that new types of animals emerged and started to compete with dinosaurs for food and stole their eggs and killed their young. Other theories suggest that disease may have killed these creatures.

Although dinosaurs were wiped out of the face of our planet 65 million years ago, they still fascinate us today. We continue to learn about them through their fossilized remains. They also live on today as birds, who are the dinosaurs' closest relatives.

OUR AMAZING WORLD

COLLECT THEM ALL

WWW.OURAMAZINGWORLDBOOKS.COM

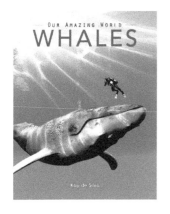

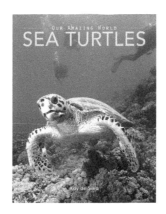

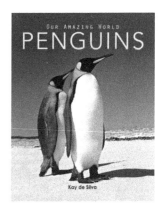

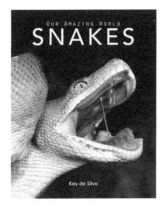

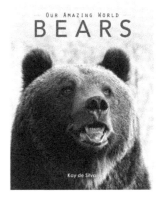

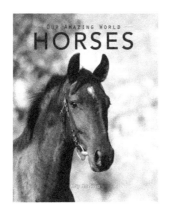

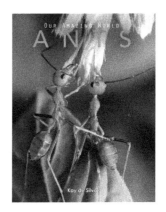

Aurora
An imprint of CKTY Publishing Solutions

www.ouramazingworldbooks.com

Text copyright © Kay de Silva, 2013
The moral right of the author has been asserted

ISBN 978-0-9946009-1-2

1, Elle Arden Images\Shutterstock; 2-3, metha1819\Shutterstock; 5, Jonfield\Bigstock; 6-7, Stephen Coburn\Shutterstock; 8-9, Digitalstudio\Bigstock; 10-11, Corey Ford\Bigstock; 12-13, 16-17, 22-23, 29, 31, Michael Rosskothen\Shutterstock; 14-15, Rojon\Bigstock; 18, bestimageservercom\Shutterstock; 19, Diomedes66\Bigstock; 20-21, Kostyantyn Ivanyshen\Shutterstock; 24, Catmando\Shutterstock; 25, Digitalstudio\Bigstock; 26, Jonfield\Bigstock; 27, AleinCat\Bigstock; 28, Miro3D\Bigstock; 30, EmeCeDesigns\Shutterstock; 34, Dariush M\Shutterstock; 32-33, Ilya Andriyanov\Shutterstock

Lightning Source UK Ltd.
Milton Keynes UK
UKHW050607141222
413813UK00013B/73